The Friedman Papers

Jeffrey Tucker

Connor Court Publishing

Published in 2018 by Connor Court Publishing Pty Ltd

Connor Court Publishing Pty Ltd
PO Box 7257
Redland Bay QLD 4165
sales@connorcourt.com
www.connorcourtpublishing.com.au

Phone 0497-900-685

Printed in Australia

ISBN: 978-1925-501-728

Front cover design: Maria Giordano

Front cover picture: Jeffrey Tucker, used with permission

This volume was compiled and edited by Nicola Wright. Connor Court, the Australian Libertarian Society (ALS) and the Australian Taxpayers Alliance (ATA) Conference would like to extend a big thank you for taking on this task at short notice. Also, a big thank you to Tim Andrews for making this project possible and allowing us to work with the ALS Friedman conference in producing this series.

Contents

1

Goodbye Net Neutrality; Hello Competition

At long last, with the end of "net neutrality," competition could soon come to the industry that delivers Internet services to you. You might be able to pick among a range of packages, some minimalist and some maximalist, depending on how you use the service. Or you could choose a package that charges based only on what you consume, rather than sharing fees with everyone else.

Internet socialism is dead; long live market forces.

With market-based pricing finally permitted, we could see new entrants to the industry because it might make economic sense for the first time to innovate. The growing competition will lead, over the long run, to innovation and falling prices. Consumers will find themselves in the driver's seat rather than crawling and begging for service and paying whatever the provider demands.

Ajit Pai, chairman of the FCC, is exactly right. "Under my proposal, the federal government will stop micromanaging the internet. Instead, the F.C.C. would simply require internet service providers to be transparent about their practices so that consumers can buy the service plan that's best for them."

A Fed for Communication

The old rules pushed by the Obama administration had locked down the industry with regulation that only helped incumbent service providers and major content delivery services. They called it a triumph of "free expression and democratic principles." It was anything but. It was actually a power grab. It created an Internet communication cartel not unlike the way the banking system works under the Federal Reserve.

Net Neutrality had the backing of all the top names in content delivery, from Google to Yahoo to Netflix to Amazon. It's had the quiet support of the leading Internet service providers Comcast and Verizon. The opposition, in contrast, had been represented by small players in the industry, hardware providers like Cisco, free-market think tanks and disinterested professors, and a small group of writers and pundits who know something about freedom and free-market economics.

The public at large should have been rising up in opposition, but people were largely ignorant of what was going on with net neutrality. Consumers imagined that they would get censorship-free access and low prices. That's not what happened.

What was sold as economic fairness and a wonderful favour to consumers was actually a sop to industrial giants. Here's what's was really going on with net neutrality. The incumbent rulers of the world's most exciting technology decided to lock down the prevailing market conditions to protect themselves against rising upstarts in a fast-changing market. The imposition of a rule against throttling content or using the market price system to allocate bandwidth resources protects against innovations that would disrupt the status quo.

Industrial Giants

What was sold as economic fairness and a wonderful favour to consumers was actually a sop to industrial giants who were seeking untrammelled access to your wallet and an end to competitive threats to market power.

Let's grasp the position of the large content providers. Here we see the obvious special interests at work. Netflix, Amazon, and the rest don't want ISPs to charge either them or their consumers for their high-bandwidth content. They would rather the ISPs themselves absorb the higher costs of such provision. It's very clear how getting the government to make price discrimination illegal is in their interest. It means no threats to their business model.

By analogy, let's imagine that a retailer furniture company were in a position to offload all their shipping costs to the trucking industry. By government decree, the truckers were not permitted to charge any more or less whether they were shipping one chair or a whole houseful of furniture. Would the furniture sellers favour such a deal? Absolutely. They could call this "furniture neutrality" and fob it off on the public as preventing control of furniture by the shipping industry.

But that leaves the question about why the opposition from the ISPs themselves (the truckers by analogy) would either be silent or quietly in favour of such a rule change. Here is where matters get complicated. After many years of experimentation in the provision of Internet services — times when we went from telephone dial-up to landlines to T1 connections to 4G and 5G data coverage — the winner in the market (for now) has been the cable companies. Consumers prefer the speed and band-width over all existing options.

But what about the future? What kind of services are going to replace the cable services, which are by-and-large monopolies due to special privileges from states and localities? It's hard to know for sure but there are some impressive ideas out there. Costs are falling for all kinds of wireless and even distributed systems.

Raising Costs

If you are a dominant player in the market — an incumbent firm like Comcast and Verizon — you really face two threats to your business model. You have to keep your existing consumer base onboard and you have to protect against upstarts seeking to poach consumers from you.

Net neutrality closed down market competition by general-ly putting government and its corporate backers in charge. For established firms, a rule like net neutrality can raise the costs of doing business, but there is a wonderful upside to this: your future potential competitors face the same costs. You are in a much better position to absorb higher costs than those barking at your heels. This means that you can slow down development, cool it on your investments in fibre optics, and generally rest on your laurels more.

But how can you sell such a nefarious plan? You get in good with the regulators. You support the idea in general, with some reservations, while tweaking the legislation in your favour. You know full well that this raises the costs to new competitors. When it passes, call it a vote for the "open internet" that will "preserve the right to communicate freely online."

Neutrality was Deceptive

But when you look closely at the effects, the reality was exactly the opposite. Net neutrality closed down market competition by generally putting government and its corporate backers in charge of deciding who can and cannot play in the market. It erected barriers to entry for upstart firms while hugely subsidizing the largest and most well-heeled content providers.

So what are the costs to the rest of us? It meant no price reductions in internet service. It could mean the opposite. Your bills went up and there was very little competition. It also meant a slowing down in the pace of technological development due to the reduction in competition that followed the imposition of this rule. In other words, it was like all government regulation: most of the costs were unseen, and the benefits were concentrated in the hands of the ruling class.

There was an additional threat: the FCC had reclassified the internet as a public utility. It meant a blank check for government control across the board. Think of the medical marketplace, which is now entirely owned by a non-competitive cartel of industry insiders. This was the future of the internet under net neutrality.

Good riddance, then. No more government-managed control of the industry. No more price fixing. No more of the largest players using government power to protect their monopoly structure.

We should take our deregulation where we can get it. In the short term, the shift by the FCC does not mean the immediate emergence of a free marketplace for Internet service. But it is a step. If we let this experiment in liberalization run a few years, we will see massive new entrants into the sector. As with every good or service provided by market forces, consumers will gain the benefit of innovation and falling prices.

The end of net neutrality is the best single deregulatory initiative yet taken by the Trump administration. The simultaneous, contradictory, and economically absurd attempt by the Justice Department to stop the merger of Time-Warner and AT&T– which might only be a government attempt to punish CNN and therefore an abuse of presidential power–is another matter for another time.

We should take our deregulation where we can get it.

2

What Really Matters about Bitcoin

After Bitcoin hit $10,000, it, at last, seemed to dawn on the mainstream financial press that this thing matters. There has been a panic rush to catch up on the meaning of it all. Some have doubled down on the claim that the whole thing is a hoax. Others dismiss it as a bubble (indeed, all financial models would suggest that a correction is needed). Some bigshots have called for it to be banned as if it is even possible to ban a mathematical protocol.

So much confusion out there! Having followed this technology from 2010, here are the ten points I find most salient about Bitcoin and the entire cryptoasset sector.

Good money emerges from exchange and entrepreneurship.

1. It was not invented by government. From the ancient world, it has been claimed that money (right and proper money) is the domain of government, at the very least to guard but also to invent, impose, and manage. In the late 19th century, an entire school of economic thought grew up around it: the State Theory of Money. Georg Friedrich Knapp's treatise by that name came out in 1905 (English translation 1924) and helped entrench the nationalization of money in central banks. Bitcoin shows that the theory is wrong. Good money emerges from exchange and entrepreneurship, as Carl Menger said.

2. It was not invented by academia. The Bitcoin protocol was released by an anonymous programmer on a small email list and then put into the commons. Economists – to say nothing of political scientists and sociologists – were entirely out of the loop. This is fascinating because mainstream intellectual hierarchy puts academia at the top and everyone else underneath. The black robes rule the course of history and everyone else is their benefactor, it is said, as if there were a structure of production for ideas. The problem with this theory emerged in the age of capitalism, when the practitioners, not the theorists, starting getting all the good ideas. Then the backlash came in the 20th century: the experts would manage society. Now we are finding out something amazing: the best ideas come from those with boots on the ground.

3. It's not all about Bitcoin. In some ways, the high-flying returns on the headline cryptocurrency are a distraction from the genius of the underlying technology: the distributed ledger called the Blockchain. This technology has spawned a financial sector just as large as Bitcoin itself, with thousands of applications, including every form of contracting. Blockchain could even lead to an upheaval in the relationship between the individual and the state. The critical thing to understand about the technology is this: it is a better way than we've ever had to document and enforce ownership claims. If you do not understand what this sentence means, I'm sorry but you do not understand the value of this technology.

Governments are an annoyance, not the authors of history.

4. The old regulations won't work. This technology is completely new, whereas all existing financial and regulatory machinery is based on muscling legacy technology to perform in a certain way. Retooling the regulations to fit simply won't work. It is only going to create messes, slowing down but not stopping, progress. Legacy bureaucracies and stakeholders will fight and fight, but nothing can stop this revolution, which is borderless and digital, making it impossible to control. Moreover, every regulation reduces competitiveness and entrenches incumbent firms. Do you think if government had banned, for example, horseshoes, electricity, internal combustion, or flight that this would have actually stopped these ideas from becoming reality? Governments are an annoyance, not the authors of history.

5. Money will be competitive. Many people see the current goings-on as a struggle between the dollar and Bitcoin. That is too simplified. The real struggle is between national money monopolies and a newly competitive system. That competition occurs between cryptocurrencies and cryptoassets. People want to know who the winner will be. This too is old-world thinking. The competitive process will never stop. Winning will be temporary, and a new challenger will rise up and take the top spot. This is a new world. No living person knows what this is like because money has been protected from market pressure for so long. In particular, Americans are going to have to get used to a world in which the dollar is no longer king.

New players are crawling out of the woodwork by the day.

6. Banking and credit will change. The whole institution of central banking is premised on the idea of a money monopoly which thereby enables full control and macroeconomic management. Crypto doesn't have to be number one in order to wreck this presumption. It only needs to bust the monopoly. With a market cap of half a trillion dollars, this might have already happened. Moreover, distributed networks weave together money and payment systems, so old-world payment processors will be next to fall. New players are crawling out of the woodwork by the day.

7. The unbanked have rights. Some people estimate that the unbanked of the world population is two billion. That is surely an underestimate. Think of the developing world but don't limit it to that. Where I live, the unbanked are everywhere, and they are that way for a variety of reasons. Maybe they fear the privacy intrusions. They have lifestyles and sources of income that fall out of the mainstream. They might have sketchy professions. Or they are too young. Maybe it is a family issue or they fear getting roped into the system. Whatever the case, they still retain economic rights, and Blockchain tech gives them options for the first time. This is the population that will fuel the entrepreneurship in this sector.

No ideology can stop this.

8. No one will be in charge. Blockchain has no central point of failure and no overarching controlling force. Financial intermediaries are not out of the picture but they are not essential. The systems of the past evolved into cartels; the systems of the future will be increasingly decentralized with non-stop disintermediation. Anyone who seeks full control will wake every day to the reality of shattered illusions. This goes for huge financial firms and also governments. Traditional policy rationale is rooted in the presumption of the pre-eminence of a single vision. The decentralized future will be rooted in the reality of nonstop disruption. No ideology can stop this.

9. It's a template for everything. Bitcoin isn't really about Bitcoin. It's about human liberty. We are not happy to live in cages of anyone's construction. The goal of human life is to find a way to freedom. Governments and their lackeys laughed and dismissed this whole revolution, circa 2009 to 2017. There is no way the bird can escape, they said. Now it is too late.

10. No one knows the future. No one could have anticipated this would happen. No one can know what lies in store for us. The future will be crowdsourced. This seeming chaos will find itself toward orderliness, and massively improve life on earth. That is how it should be.

2

How to Live Like a Bitcoin Millionaire

The opportunity is to live every dream you have ever had. Now. The problem is that for every dream you realize, you have to relinquish some of your property. And every bit of that property is hard to come by, extraordinarily lucrative, and the single most in-demand thing on the planet earth.

Among the crypto rich, it's hip to be poor. You must be tight. Stingy. No signs of wealth. So, yes, you could be living it up. Instead, you have become addicted to seeing your net worth rise and rise…oh, and rise further, and further, and rise again. And more. The only trick is not to die before you do something with it. That seems pretty easy, for the most part.

What You Spend Today

Here is the problem with using (as versus merely saving) Bitcoin. There are no lack of options for how to spend (sell) it. But you do that, and then you don't have it. You spend $1. That's $2 you won't have in maybe one month. You spend $50K on a car. Wow, that could have otherwise turned into $100K and you could have bought two cars. Then instead of a money-earning thing, you have a stupid car that just gets you from here to there same as your previous car. So you decide to drive the old thing, as supposedly embarrassing as it is.

Your next car will be a Tesla. You could throw down for one today and not feel it. But that $75K expenditure becomes $100K you will not otherwise have in a few months, maybe. Too risky. It's better to take the bus.

It's the same with dressing well. Honestly, who even cares? Every stitch of clothing is money that could be earning money in your crypto wallet, spun gold like Rapunzel's hair, except that the strands keep growing. So you wear your old jeans, hoodies, and sneakers left over from the last time you splurged 24 months ago.

Ideal Expenditure: Zero

Among the crypto rich, it's hip to be poor. You must be tight. Stingy. No signs of wealth. You could give to charity, but why? In six months, your gift could be multiplied by five times. You can become a beloved benefactor of great causes. Someday. Surely the charity will make it until then.

Even better, show signs of poverty. You shop at Walmart, thrift stores, and sell every stupid thing you have on eBay – why did we buy so much stuff in the past? – so that you can buy more crypto. You brag to everyone at how little you spend on anything at all. Every bargain is a badge of honour. You will not get lunch. You kidding me? That's $9 that will soon turn to $18 and buy two lunches. Why would anyone do that?

Forget fat and happy. Crypto millionaires are emaciated and penurious.

They are called the HODLers, the people who forego today's consumption for…something tomorrow. Sure, the money will go somewhere. Maybe it is a yacht. Maybe a home. Maybe even that Maserati. Endless travel to…New Zealand, which is the only place people really want to go anyway. Dream on.

In the meantime, you are addicted to the habit of turning all income to crypto, living like a pauper, looking like heck, staying away from the malls and the first-class tickets.

You have never been richer in your life. You have never lived poorer.

In the Bitcoin community, you dare not show signs of wealth. Someone might think you are poor.

Magic Internet Money has become the real thing, if by real you mean digits on a computer screen. You could go to the movies but that is folly. Wait a week and you can torrent the thing and watch on your iPhone— if it is not busy mining Bitcoin Platinum. Or maybe you give in and go once, but you sneak in your own beer and popcorn because who wants to pay those prices?

Remember the old days when Bitcoin was $350? People lived it, spending like crazy on liquor, fast cars, temporary romantic partners, and dancing on boats. What were they thinking? If they had done differently, these people would have been billionaires, not merely millionaires. Never make that mistake again. If you have to buy something, make it CryptoKitties.

What's Really Real

Magic Internet Money has become the real thing, if by real you mean digits on a computer screen. The digits are all that matter. It's zero after zero, added while you sleep. There is nothing in this room that compares. Nothing on this city block. Nothing in this city. All physical things kind of look ridiculous. The only reality is virtual.

Think back to the great inflation of the Weimar period when the spenders were savvy and the savers were chumps. The irresponsible knew the score and the prudent old-worlders languished in ignorance of the new times. The whole of society turned upside down. The culture of thrift became a culture of panicked consumption.

And why? Because the money failed. It was caused by extreme inflation that devoured savings in a short period of time and led even to starvation. Here is what hyperinflation can do when there are no real options to nationalized money.

Repudiate Profligacy

Well, the great Bitcoin bull market is the opposite. This is the crypto deflation in which the monetary unit becomes ever more valuable in terms of goods and services — if there should ever come a time when people actually spend the stuff. Society is turned upside down, yet again, to become a world in which the frugal rule and those who spend just don't know what's what. It's the perfect foil to a century of inflation.

It's a new way to live, one that repudiates profligacy in all its forms. Weimar led to Hitler. The great global crypto deflation will lead to something else. Maybe it will be freedom. It is building a new class based not on inheritance or privilege but merit and savings. These people have stolen nothing. Instead, they have put their faith in something new, and not just a new technology. It's a new way to live, one that repudiates profligacy in all its forms.

People say that Bitcoin enthusiasts are banking on an illusion. Maybe it is the opposite. Maybe it is they who have finally embraced the core truth that what you spend today only eats up potential wealth tomorrow. After 100 years of bad money, that truth has evaporated from public consciousness. Bitcoin reveals it anew.

This might be the real lasting legacy of the blockchain technological revolution: the restoration of frugality as the basis of wealth-building from which the whole of society will benefit.

4

The Best Defence against Sexual Harassment is a Free Labour Market

Lin Farley, the person who coined the phrase "sexual harassment" in 1975, is today deeply unhappy about the movement she started. She thinks it has flopped.

"At first," she writes, "it felt as if the term had the potential to change everything. Working women immediately took up the phrase, which finally captured the sexual coercion they were experiencing daily."

It's true that by giving the practice a name, she writes, the rules in corporate life and government began to change. Training programs against sexual harassment are common. Women with some degree of professional success, resources, and other options have new ways to seek redress. The law changed. Lawyers have won big.

She is less convinced that much has changed in practice for the average woman professional. Coining the phrase "has done far less to encourage the conversations I had envisioned back in 1975 that I believed would help to change our culture," she writes. "Worse, it allows those who would argue that the culture and power dynamics have changed to fall back on the new rules as evidence."

Laws Don't Work

This is hardly the first time that new laws failed to achieve the hoped-for effect. Her proposed solution? Beyond recommending more talk, more exposure, more #metoo hashtags, she doesn't seem to have one, beyond writing furious opinion articles for the *New York Times*.

More government involvement only means fighting coercion with more coercion—not a very promising path.

It's about an economy in which no one is trapped, imposed upon, or forced by lack of options to endure personal degradation. My alternative proposition: the best possible defence against all forms of exploitation at the workplace, including that which takes a gendered or sexualized form, is a free market in labour. Laws, mandates, and regulations that lock people into particular jobs, industries, and career paths make workers more vulnerable to abuse from bosses. The best way to equalize power between owners/managers and employees is a highly competitive labour market.

The further we move from the free market, the more the exploitation of labour is a major problem.

Let's specify here that there will never be nirvana. This world will never be a place of universal holy decency. Trolls, jerks, and exploitative bosses will always be with us. The real question is: how can the power that bad people have over good people be reduced in a way that results in the least-possible harm to people and society? At minimum, victims and potential victims need a way to escape. The escape route should be obvious, low cost, and not injurious.

This is about more than the right to quit and get a new job. It's about establishing an intensely rivalrous market for labour, such that employers have to be decent people to get and retain workers. They have to behave or lose talent to their competitors. Money talks, instructs, and trains people to be better people. It's about an economy in which no one is trapped, imposed upon, or forced by lack of options to endure personal degradation.

The Capitalist Way

Providing such an escape was central to the liberal revolution of the 18th century: no serfdom, no slavery, no servitude. The result was capitalism, the only system of economics ever actually to eliminate the role of exploitation in labour and capital relations (Marx had it exactly backwards).

Look at what Ludwig von Mises wrote in 1927 about the power of labour vs. the power of capital in a free market:

> In a private enterprise, the hiring of labour is not the conferring of a favour, but a business transaction from which both parties, employer and employee, benefit. The employer must Endeavor to pay wages corresponding in value to the labour performed. If he does not do this, he

runs the risk of seeing the worker leave his employment for that of a better-paying competitor. The employee, in order not to lose his job, must in his turn endeavour to fulfil the duties of his position well enough to be worth his wages. Since employment is not a favour, but a business transaction, the employee does not need to fear that he may be discharged if he falls into personal disfavour. For the entrepreneur who discharges, for reasons of personal bias, a useful employee who is worth his pay harms only himself and not the worker, who can find a similar position elsewhere.

Sounds beautiful, right? Exactly. The ideal here sounds fantastic, if we would get around to practicing it. Mises immediately turns to the problem of intervention in the free market. All interventions create bureaucratic forms of management to supplant market forces. This reduces real labour rights – even when it takes place in the name of labour rights.

What are the interventions that have reduced labour rights and given bosses the sense that they are not engaged in business deals so much as "granting favours" to workers on a quid pro quo basis? The list is long but includes health care mandates, mandatory vacation times, the costs of payroll taxation, professional licensure, minimum wages, and the long list of so-called "labour rights" that only end in trapping workers in jobs from which they can't walk away.

All these programs stifle competition in the labour market. They make workers less marketable and cause people to cling to the jobs they have. To put a fine point on it: Obamacare contributed massively to enabling sexual harassment.

Job Lock

Think of your own case. If you walked out of your job today, how long do you suppose it would take to get another? How long would you expect to be without income? In some service industries like restaurants, hotels, and bars, it usually takes a few weeks. But once you enter into more high-end positions, matters become grim. It can take six weeks to two months to land another position.

Termination severance, by tradition from days of old, provides for only two weeks of income. Then you have the huge problem of health care. The timer starts right away. You will have to go to the misnamed "marketplace" dominated by Obamacare or pay a penalty to the government. Then you might have to move, and that is expensive. Meanwhile you are trying to line up interviews and make a good impression – even while you are panicked about your life, social status, and finances as never before.

You look at all of this and think:

Yeah, I think I'll keep my job. True, my boss is a jerk. He creeps me out. He's got all kinds of issues. My manager was making vague insinuations that make me uncomfortable. He explodes abusively just to show his power. My supervisor is trolling my social media and asking personal questions that are none of his business. But what can I do? No one wants to face unemployment.

Job lock of this sort is a major reason for the disproportionate power that bosses have over workers. It is a major contributing factor that enables and perpetuates exploitation. The more choice exists in the labour marketplace, the more workers are in a position to demand decency, respect, and decorum from management.

Please Come Back

Some years ago, back when the economy was growing fast and companies were desperate for workers, I witnessed a scene in a convenience store I will never forget. A young worker came in a few minutes late for work. The boss was furious with her and started yelling at her, in front of customers. His face was turning red.

She stood there taking it all in. When he was done, she calmly took off her badge and put it on the counter. She said "goodbye" and walked out the front door.

What do you suppose happened? Immediately the bossman realized what a jerk he was being. He went flying out the door to stop her. He begged her to come back. I couldn't hear the conversation, but he seemed to bring her around. Apologies, raises, better hours, promises not to be a jerk – I can't say for sure what it was. But whatever he said persuaded her to come back and start work.

A free market means progress toward ending all forms of exploitation, including sexual harassment. I watched this scene with a sense of awe. There we have it, the picture of an ideal! The labour contract is an exchange in which both parties benefit. If one party wants out, the deal is over. No one is ever harmed. No one is ever humiliated. No one should ever have to face the problem of providing any kind of quid pro quo services that are not in the contract. Fairness, decency, and humane values win.

A free market means progress toward ending all forms of exploitation, including sexual harassment, indecency, inappropriate touching, casting couches, lunches that last too long and become too intimate, suggestive texts, late-night personal communications, invasive interrogations of personal lives, star chambers, subtle or not-subtle intimidations, or any other form of imposition. The path to peace and human dignity is the same here as everywhere else: make all things voluntary.

You say that this will not finally put an end to the problem? It won't. But it gives us the best possible way to improve our lives and diminish human suffering. That's more than can be achieved any laws, op-eds, shaming, or far-flung hopes for humanity to improve on its own.

5

Of Course the Alt-Right
is Against Capitalism

Some people on the left are starting to worry about getting trolled by the alt-right. This is because the alt-right has become aggressively anti-capitalist, pro-welfare state, and in favour of a government that specifically promotes white interests, not a free market that offers no privilege to anyone.

"The alt-right is looking to expand its ranks," declares *Salon*, "and prominent leaders of the notorious white supremacist movement apparently believe that leftists are an ideal target for their recruiting efforts." This follows a huge investigative piece that appeared in *The Nation*, in which a reporter from the publication attended a number of alt-right events, where leftist ideas are newly fashionable.

Salon then warns leftists not to fall for it:

The alt-right's "anti-capitalism," then, is really just anti-Semitism wrapped up in an economic veil, devoid of any real critique of capitalism. Their economic turn is simply a means to further their movement and spread their racist ideology.

There is truth in that statement. Anti-Semitism and racism have been a core part of the attacks on the market for centuries, which raises some interesting questions about the anti-market left itself.

The *Salon* claim also understates the full-on anti-liberalism of alt-right ideology, a topic that forms the thesis of my book on the topic. Indeed, in its origins, this outlook was formed in opposition to the world-transforming power of markets. It is rooted in resentment of the expansion of liberty and prosperity of the early 19th century, and the fear that capitalism would break down old hierarchies, traditional attachments, and national borders. The revolt they favoured was always a revolt against the market.

Trolling the Left

It's true that in modern times, in the United States, this gang gained public attention by first attempting to pass themselves off as libertarians, hanging out at meet ups, conferences, and taking over subreddits. It worked for a while, given the libertarian commitment to free association and free speech. But then people got wise to the game. Over the last year, many leaders within the libertarian community have doubled down on an effort to preserve the integrity of libertarian ideas and make sure they were not compromised by this gang.

Libertarianism then became a low performer for recruitment. That's when the shift became apparent. The new language of the alt-right is all about denouncing corporate capitalism for failing to do its bidding. They say that capitalism is too politically correct, is excluding them from social media, is declining to let them use financial tools to raise money, and is generally promoting their enemies in cooperation with the media.

The left often accuses capitalism of doing things for which it is not actually guilty, such as excluding the poor, exploiting workers, ravaging the earth, and so on. The alt-right, however, is mostly attacking capitalism for things that corporations are, in fact, doing and doing well. These people are not popular people, and their views have proven poisonous for venues like Twitter and Facebook, and are banned not for PC reasons, but simply because they reduce the value of the platforms.

In other ways, however, the market – which is no respecter of persons or ideologies – has been a great friend to the alt-right. Amazon sells their books. Their podcasts are hosted by capitalist firms. Their publishing venues are based on the profit-and-loss model. The market has done the same for red and green ideologies too. The market is a tool for everyone without exception.

Tribal Barriers

It's also true that the market has always provided a main impetus for breaking down tribal barriers. It thinks in terms of individual rights because it is designed to appeal to individual minds. If your goal is the promotion of group solidarity and exclusion, it is not a good tool. Its watchwords are inclusion and empowerment of everyone. It was the gradual liberalization of markets and the technology and universalist values that came with it that ended slavery, promoted minority and women's rights, and created this thing we call the middle class.

It makes perfect sense, then, that the alt-right would reveal itself to be anti-liberal not just in politics, but also in economics. In fact, it should make the left uncomfortable that the alt-right feels at home with the economic ideas of socialists, and not for the first time. What has always united the Hegelians of the right and left has been their shared opposition to the free society. The details of the critique and proposed alternatives are different depending on the tribe, but that economic freedom itself is the target of both is nothing new.

Recall that in its early days, the Nazi party called merely for boycotts of Jewish businesses, and even instructed party members to use no physical violence. This was April 1, 1933. The hope was that this would inspire a nation to cause bankruptcy to the Jews and drive them out of the country. It didn't work. People continued to deal with Jewish doctors, grocers, and intellectuals. The next step was absolutely necessary: the Nazis abolished the market itself with the Nuremberg Laws of 1935. History has shown us that if any tribe seeks to control the market, they will have to abolish it first.

The Blending of Left and Right

The alt-right's turn toward overt anti-capitalism is neither surprising nor new nor counterintuitive. The revolving door between the left and the right has been going around for two centuries. People like John Ruskin or Thomas Carlyle might have been non-Marxists and conservatives in every respect, but they targeted the market as the most feared enemy of their agenda for social and economic control. The Progressives too, split between their right and left branches, each anxious to use the state to stop the market drive that spreads the benefits of prosperity to all people.

The strange way in which the far left and right are bound up with each other has been noted by consistent liberals for a long time. Their membership is fluid, wrote Max Eastman in 1956, observing that "every judgment and choice, every trait and mode of behaviour, that once had given meaning to the word 'Right' is now supported and approved by those whom all agree in calling 'Left' or 'Leftist.'"

Equally, there have been periods in history when what used to be called left was suddenly called right, as illustrated in the magically adaptive mind of Werner Sombart, who easily made the journey from Communist to Nazi.

In the much-truncated and cartoonish remake in the presidential election of 2016, many observers noted the odd way in which it was difficult to distinguish the platforms of Bernie Sanders and Donald Trump: anti-trade, pro-"worker", promising universal health coverage, and generally railing against globalism and capitalist financial power. That they hated each other was not a surprise. This fits the narrative of history in which political tribes save their most vituperative attacks for those closest to them in outlook.

(Fortunately for the American people, the winner of that election has come to discover that deregulation and tax cuts are more popular among the public than protectionism and executive centralization.)

The alt-right's turn toward overt anti-capitalism is neither surprising nor new nor counterintuitive. It doesn't just stem from anti-Semitism, even if that is a seemingly inevitable part of it. Collectivism of all sorts and every form stands opposed to economic liberty. Just give it time: all types of collectivism end up sounding more or less like each other.

6

History is Malleable in the Land of the Dead

We tend to think of the past as settled. There is nothing we can do to change it. But this is not entirely true. How we think about the past – the good guys and bad guys, the justice and injustice, the causes and effects – has a profound effect on our perceptions of the present. Our understanding comes to be revised based on new information as it comes to light. In this sense, the past is not settled. It is a living reality.

Big thoughts, right? They come to me courtesy of an animated film now rocking the theatres. I've felt for years that there is more genuinely adult content in the best of the movies made for kids than in most "adult" fare. The film introduces us into a land of the dead – neither time nor eternity – and raises the challenging idea that the dead, too, are still learning and changing.

Philosophy of History

This exciting story takes place on many levels. The movie in question is Pixar's new animated feature *Coco*. It explores a realm of the culture, religion, and nationality of Mexico. It received its theatrical premiere in Mexico on the Día de Muertos (Day of the Dead) and was released to US audiences later. All the voice actors are Mexican.

This exciting story takes place on many levels. As soon as you think it is a feel-good tribute to family loyalty, it takes you to another place completely, to explore something as profound as the philosophy of history. This was the part that stunned me and left me thinking hard.

It follows the young life of Miguel Rivera, who feels the calling to be a musician but faces resistance from his family. His great-great grandfather was a musician who left his family to pursue a dream of becoming a great performer, writing music and singing for the world. His family was so bitter about his decision that two generations banned music from the household in favour of the family business of shoemaking.

But Miguel doesn't want to be a shoemaker. He wants to sing and play music like his great-great grandfather. So on the Day of the Death, he makes his way to a monument to the famous singer Ernesto de la Cruz. He picks up the singer's guitar and suddenly finds himself transported to another world entirely. It is the land of the dead.

Cool City

It turns out that the land of the dead is a happening place with great transportation systems, colourful apartment units, great places to eat and drink, and even pop stars and concerts. In order to get back to the land of the living, Miguel has to seek the blessing of an ancestor who resides there. He finds his great-great grandmother, but she will only give her blessing with the condition that Miguel decline to sing music. It's an offer that Miguel cannot accept.

Once forgotten, the dead finally die and go away to nowhere in particular forever. Gradually we come to learn who lives in this place and why. It's where you go when you die but the amount of wealth you possess and the length of time you get to stay there is entirely dependent on whether you are actively remembered by your survivors. The day when this takes place is the Day of the Dead, during which time mementos of one's dead ancestors should be displayed so that they can continue to live it up in the land of the dead. Once forgotten, the dead finally die and go away to nowhere in particular forever.

That's pretty harsh! And this is precisely why it is imperative that families continue to revere dead family members.

Here is where the drama gets interesting. Miguel decides to seek out another dead family member who can send him back to the land of the living without the annoying condition that he not sing and play. He seizes on the famous singer Ernesto de la Cruz, who he believes to be his real great-great grandfather. He is so well remembered among the living that Ernesto is extremely wealthy.

However, we gradually come to learn that he is something of a jerk. The people in the land of the dead come to learn this too, once they discover a hidden secret in his life. The popular image of this guy is shattered and he loses his fan base completely, which is a hilarious turn given that all these people are dead!

What Does this Mean?

This is where the philosophy of history comes to matter. The reputations of the dead are subject to change as both the living and the dead develop new opinions in light of new information. This ongoing learning process shifts culture and society in both the land of the dead and the living. What a remarkable tribute to the power of stories that we know and tell each other!

An example from real life might be someone like Woodrow Wilson. He was revered after his death as an intellectual, a great statesman, a bringer of peace, a prophet of democracy and nationalism. Today, matters are different. Wilson is known as a proponent of eugenics, a champion of the Klan, a hard-core racist, a tool of the ruling class, and a bringer of murderous and pointless war.

What a difference! And all of this while he lived in the land of the dead!

The past is not settled. It continues to live and, therefore, change. Or consider FDR. To this day, he is seen as the man who save us from the Great Depression even though he evidently did not. He is regarded as a champion of the downtrodden even though he was the architect of the corporate state that cartelized and locked down economic growth. And like Wilson, his views on matters of race and demographics trended white supremacist and exclusionary. When will FDR's reputation change? Surely it is coming.

Or think of a president like Andrew Jackson. He is now seen as an opponent of the national bank and a champion of the people. But what happens when he comes to be seen as an exterminator of the native population, a demagogue who ran a corrupt presidency, and an unscrupulous pusher of military imperialism?

This could happen, but it depends on the people who dig up the facts and get them marketed to the population. The past is not settled. It continues to live and, therefore, change. And it changes our impression of the present.

Stealing Ideas

Coco offers other fascinating insight into the whole area of intellectual property and cultural appropriation. The big issue in the land of the dead concerns who precisely wrote the famous songs that Ernesto de la Cruz sings. He has always claimed credit, but is this correct? When the verdict changes, his reputation also changes.

I wondered at first if we were going to get a lecture on attribution rights from Hollywood, but this is not what it's about. It's about whether to respect the merely famous or the people who are the real creators. You can respect "creative rights" and the need for proper attribution without passing laws such as intellectual property.

As for cultural appropriation, the movie might at first seem to dabble in the current fashion for cultures to wall themselves off and protect their products from being "stolen" by others. Actually, and fortunately, there is nothing particularly "political correct" about this film. It is a straight up celebration of Mexican culture and the myths that have shaped it.

Who has appropriated whom? It runs both directions, as it always does when two cultures come in contact with each other. I recognized so much of this from my own childhood, when my best friend was a first-generation child of immigrants from across the border. Their lives were so different from mine. That house across the street became a window into another beautiful world and served as a constant reminder that my family's way was not the only way. I marvelled at the Mayan calendar on the wall, the method that Mama Rede used to make nightly tortillas, the luxuriously Latinate language, and the family rituals.

To me, it was all so liberating.

Watching Coco, I was struck so hard by the magical way in which Mexican culture so beautifully blended two religious traditions, the faith of the Aztec heritage and European-style Catholicism, into a seamless whole. The Day of the Dead becomes All Souls, the need to remember our ancestors becomes prayers for the dead from Catholic liturgy, and the land of the dead is a proxy for Purgatory.

Who has appropriated whom? It runs both directions, as it always does when two cultures come in contact with each other. The bottom line is that there would be no such thing as a Mexican culture to celebrate had it not been for cultural appropriation.

The movie Coco is so infectious that it would not surprise me if it inspires many young people to appropriate aspects of that culture for themselves.

As for its philosophy of history, the film is right: the past is never stable, nor should it be.

7

Dropping Traffic Rules and Signs Would Make Us Safer

This morning, I was sitting at a stop light and heard a terrifying screeching. A black sedan headed my direction from the oncoming lane was careening across six lanes of traffic, with squealing brakes and tires, through the intersection, flying forward some 75 or so yards and finally landing against a pole with a mighty impact. Terror shot through everyone in the vicinity.

Green means go. The problem was that there were cars in the way. What happened? The woman behind the wheel had been driving 45 mph and saw a green light ahead of her. Green means go. The problem was that there were cars in the way. By the time she took note of this, it was too late. She swerved into the next lane and lost control of her car. Even an hour later, there were still police cars, fire engines, and ambulances everywhere. It was very bad, but it could have been much worse.

She should have been more alert, of course. But like most drivers, her attention was entirely on the fact that the green light gave her the right of way, regardless of what was around her. Green gives her the legal right to drive forward. It doesn't guarantee that doing so will be safe.

Traffic engineers need to rig the signalling system to let people know that most basic condition of driving: for your sake and others, be safe. Increasingly, in Europe, they are addressing the problem in an unusual way: fewer lights, stops, rules, and signals are better than more. Some cities are eliminating signs and signals at major intersections completely, based on the realization that individual, on-the-ground rationality works better than top-down rules.

Traffic and Liberty

In the 1960s, when libertarianism as a political outlook was coming into its own, people made lots of fun of our obsession with laws and rules. They said that instead of saving civilization from barbarians, we spent all our time kvetching about the stop sign down the street.

Modern traffic theory is coming around to the view that signs, rules, and instructions have made the roads far less safe. It is funny caricature. But every caricature contains truth. Stop signs and traffic lights, on public property and enforced by agents of the state, can in fact have grimly coercive features. I rolled through one once, got a ticket, forgot to pay it, and found myself arrested during Sunday brunch. As I languished in jail, I was given a poignant illustration of the maxim that every law is ultimately enforced at the point of a gun.

Here's what's interesting: it seems that libertarians did not in fact spend *enough* time kvetching about stop signs. Modern traffic theory is coming around to the view that signs, rules, and instructions have made the roads far less safe. When you remove them, the results point to a paradox: the less you tell people what to do, the better people are at figuring it out for themselves.

Vox, which is known as a centre-left political publication, has made an interesting film about this theory in practice. They present it as a purely engineering point. Drivers need visual cues to govern how fast they are going. These cues are called "edge friction." If you eliminate them all, traffic speeds up and drivers become less interested in and cautious about possible signs of danger around them. But when you add random cues all around– pedestrians, drivers of all sorts going every which way–people become attentive to others.

With shared space and no formal rules, everyone stays on the move but with a sense of navigating obstacles. This can have the effect of causing traffic overall to navigate the space better.

Maybe you have experienced this before in your town. The main light in the town centre is a major clog on all days. Then one day the electricity blasts their functionality. Drivers intuitively turn it into a causal four-way stop. For the first time ever, there is no clog.

Everyone stays on the move but with caution.

The Bigger Implications

The video doesn't go into it but consider the implications of the American system of red lights and green lights. The case I saw this morning illustrates the point. How many times have you had a clear lane with a red light that suddenly turns green? We naturally think that this means that we are safe to step on the gas. If there were no light at all, we would approach the situation very differently.

If street intersections function better without top-down management and imposition, what about the rest of the social order? So it is with the texting and driving problem. Drivers need a reason to stop texting, something more than a law. If roads really were multiuse and filled with uncertainty, people would have to start paying attention rather than merely complying with signs and rules. They would have to engage their brains with the task at hand.

The texting-while-driving problem stems from the perception that the rules, signs, and signals keep us safe, so why not find something else to pay attention to, such as my social feed? If we drivers had an ongoing job to do, the incentives would change completely.

The Vox video only frustrated me for failing to draw out the larger implications of the discovery that evolving patterns of adaptive behaviour are more socially functional than laws and signs. In other words, the more that systems are structured to elicit the decentralized intelligence of drivers, the more likely they are to serve human welfare.

That's the broader point about this microcosm that has

gigantic implications about the macrocosm. If street intersections function better without top-down management and imposition, what about the rest of the social order? There are other forms of accidents, wrecks, and pile-ups going on every day in the business world, all due to too much coercive management rather than trusting people to figure things out on their own.

F.A. Hayek's main point against central planning is that it is impossible for minds operating outside the system to outthink the decentralized knowledge that is embedded in the social process of discovery, with its constantly changing conditions, multitudinous minds at work, and huge diffusion of plans. What emerges in a state of freedom are adaptive institutions and rules of thumb that make society function better than laws and legislation.

The gradual realization of a better way to manage traffic has implications that go far beyond how well cars navigate the intersection down the street. It should tell us something much larger: liberty always works better than social and economic engineering managed from legislatures and bureaucracies. It's not just about "edge friction"; it's about life philosophy.

8

Are You a Genius or a Fraud?

One time, when I was a small child, I saw Hank Aaron go to bat. He had already hit his 500th home run. I was looking forward to seeing this genius do his thing. I was devastated when he struck out. Some genius, I recall thinking. As an eight-year-old, my first thought was that I could have done exactly what he did.

Of course, Hank knew something that I, at the time, did not. Genius is about averages, not every time at bat. If every time you strike out, you imagine that you might be a fraud, you will make yourself insane.

The best ball player I knew as a kid dropped out because he couldn't handle the constant seesawing between being loved and hated by teammates and the crowd, depending on the last play. One minute, team members are carrying you around as a hero, and the parents are cheering. The next play had to be great yet again else everyone would be devastated and disappointed. You would be shunned. No victory lasts. It's just part of the game, but

51

this kid wanted out and eventually went into a profession where the pressure wasn't so intense.

And yet, the problem of constantly deciding whether we are great or terrible at what we do, toying with the belief that we are geniuses just before worrying that we will be exposed as frauds, is just part of life.

Your Post Is Stupid

Some people are crippled by the fear of getting it wrong and never say anything. You can experience this on social media any day. You research a topic, develop a solid opinion on it, post it, only to have people point out your abysmal ignorance minutes later. Oddly, our critics are often right about us: there is a point we didn't know or we overlooked. Maybe it doesn't change the outcome of our opinion, but we surely should have known this before posting.

Some people are crippled by the fear of getting it wrong and never say anything. Some people become enormously accomplished but never quite believe it. They are victims of what is called the Imposter Syndrome, which is the belief that every achievement is really just a lucky break or a benefit from the ignorance of one's peers or that we have temporarily pulled the wool over people's eyes.

In my experience, it is more common that people toggle between belief that they are great and then terrible, great then terrible, over and over again, before finally settling into a belief that we are all something in between.

Am I a Star or a Fraud?

A good example comes from an account of a man who competed as a pianist in the amateur Van Cliburn contest in the 1990s. In his account,

> I haven't felt this nervous before any recital and tell myself that I should be confident, having already made it through the previous rounds. But I can't shake the fear that I'm a fraud who lucked into the finals while all the other finalists are pros, even if they're called amateurs. An extra degree of scrutiny directed at me is attributable to the conspicuous nature of my profession [journalist], which is no consolation at the moment. Reverse psychology – I'm not a fraud, I'm a star – doesn't help, either. Star, fraud – the only thing I conclude is that I should be focusing on the music.

That article appeared in 1999, and the passage above is the one that stood out to me. It signifies that search that all of us make to define a sense of precisely who we are based on our skill level and, in turn, what to expect from others in their treatment of us. Mostly, however, it works in the opposite direction. We extract information from what others around us say about us and infuse that sense into our self-perceptions.

Just like in little league baseball, this happens to everyone throughout life. You do something amazing, and everyone sings your praises. But now you have a new problem: expectations are newly high for your performance. This is especially true if you have won or received a promotion or raise: now you have to get out there and kill it every time, else you will be seen as undeserving.

There's an added problem to being perceived as a genius. Others will want to tear you down and revel in your fall. Envy is the most hidden but most deeply dangerous of the deadly sins. Those whom envy victimizes are almost always surprised because they were expecting their achievement to be followed by accolades and promotion, not resentment and nefarious plots. But the only way fully to avoid envy is intolerable: never be excellent.

Ignore Everyone

One solution is to do your best to shut out external stimuli. Michael Scott of The Office is, as usual, wrong. He says, "Don't listen to your critics, only listen to your fans." That's classic Scott: arrogant, obtuse, unself-aware of the absurdity of what he is saying.

A priest friend of mine gave better advice. He told me to listen to my critics, not my fans. The second part about not listening to fans is essential to not having an inflated and unsustainable perception of yourself as a genius. It also keeps you humble. The first part about listening to your critics, however, can be demoralizing if you take it too far – especially if you are active on Twitter.

We have a bad habit of believing that greatness is embodied in one actor, one mind, one life. Here, the priest is echoing St. Augustine:

> It's easy enough to think about grandeur, easy enough to enjoy honours, easy enough to give our ears to yes-men and flatterers. To put up with abuse, to listen patiently to reproaches, to pray for the insolent, this is the Lord's cup, this is sharing the Lord's table.

Another solution strikes me as balanced. What if all of us are both geniuses in some respects and frauds in other respects? What if all of us are a mix of both? This strikes me as an answer that is consistent with the observation of F.A. Hayek that true genius is both individual and social. They are mutually dependent and inextricably linked. In the same way, the perception that we are frauds is nothing but the sudden realization of the imperfectability of the human personality in the face of the kaleidic uncertainty of time. Both are true.

No One Mind

On the point about genius, we have a bad habit of believing that greatness is embodied in one actor, one mind, one life. But Thomas Carlyle was just wrong: no man is so great as to earn him the right to rule his fellows.

Nor do we find unique geniuses in the history of invention. Despite the high reputations of the Wright Brothers, Alexander Graham Bell, and Eli Whitney, there is in fact an ongoing dispute about who was first in flight, who invented the telephone, and whether the cotton gin was actually improved much at all by Whitney's machine.

Historians of invention have yet to discover any innovations that were genuinely the product of a single mind. What we find again and again is the phenomenon of Multiple Discovery, with many people competing for the title of the first. It is for this reason that Nobel Prizes are increasingly given to teams of researchers. It seems more accurate to say that genius is in the air and perceived by many different people in different places, even if they have never had contact with each other.

Keep looking for the prophets, the soothsayers, the fortune-tellers, and we pay them a healthy sum when they have the right scientific credentials. There are grave dangers associated with attributing the title of genius to anyone. Remember how after 2008 there was a hunt to find out who "predicted the crisis" and then follow their stock picks? We should have done the opposite, found the people who predicted it and then ignored everything they said afterwards. They were almost universally wrong about the follow-up. It can be hard to distinguish the perfect prediction from the broken clock that is correct twice a day.

I recall having almost perfectly predicted the date on which the Bitcoin price would hit $1,000. A wise person called me and said: "Don't ever try this trick again. You can predict a price or a date but never both." Sure enough, Bitcoin soon fell to $350. No, I didn't predict that. Was I a genius or a fraud? Maybe, just like everyone else, I had some perceptive insight and then didn't successfully or reliably repeat it.

All Certainty Is Fraudulent

Hayek showed us that individual genius is not necessary. The highest forms of intelligence do not live in individuals' minds but in social processes and institutions that no single human mind can fully conceptualize. The result is an order that no man can accurately comprehend or describe, much less design. This is precisely the core of his defence of freedom: we need this process to be adaptable to become ever smarter and more reflective of a multitude of intelligences that emerge from human action.

Where does that leave us as individuals? All we can hope to do is precisely what the pianist quoted above says: "I should be focusing on the music." That is to say, do the best we can on the task in which we are engaged. You will have moments of genius and moments of failure, sometimes home runs and sometimes strikeouts, good performances and bad. Knowing this is neither a complex nor a syndrome; it is the stuff of life.

The most successful musicians I've known are not the best; it's just that they work harder to become successful. The "natural talents" among us rarely blossom because they don't have to work at it. At the same time, seeming disabilities become abilities because they motivate us to overcome them.

Be quick and excited to recognize the genius you find in others. You know what I personally believe is the best way to avoid this angst-filled toggling between exaggerations on both ends of the psychological spectrum? Be happy to improve yourself and the world around you in whatever way you can every day. Stop comparing yourself against the phony impressions others give of their lives on social media.

Be quick and excited to recognize the genius you find in others. We are all made of the same stuff with the same capacity for high achievement in some realms and failures in others. Working together, we can't make ourselves and the world perfect, but we can make them better and more beautiful.

That should be enough.

9

The Red Politics of Revenge

I saw the movie Reds when it came out in 1981, and I still re-watch it to this day. After all these years, the movie holds up as one of the most intellectually interesting and visually powerful portrayals of lost history that I've seen.

The movie stars Warren Beatty playing John Reed, the famous communist journalist who wrote Ten Days that Shook the World, a journalistic account of the Bolshevik revolution that whipped up a great deal of sympathy for the Bolsheviks in the United States. Diane Keaton plays his girlfriend and eventual wife, Louise Bryant.

Emma Goldman tries to talk some sense into Reed in the years following and explains that millions have died from starvation. The film is unforgettable in so many ways. It includes some of the best romantic fight scenes I've ever seen, not least because they paralleled the actual off-screen lives of Beatty and Keaton. The portrayals of figures like Max Eastman, Eugene

O'Neill, and Emma Goldman are very convincing.

In terms of culture and politics, the film provides a richer education than you can get from 50 books on the topic of the Progressive Era, the Great War, the Russian Revolution, and the heady brew of interwoven cultural issues like women's suffrage, birth control, abortion, free love, and the beginnings of the organized socialist movement in the United States.

The account of the many splits on the American Left in those days helps people understand why the history of the I.W.W. (Wobblies) is something that needs to be understood.

I've never been sympathetic to the Bolsheviks as versus the old regime in Russia, but the scenes here from the revolution are completely inspired and touch the heart of anyone who agrees with Jefferson on the positive need for revolution from time to time. The portrayals of both Lenin and Trotsky seem authentic, and thrillingly so.

That sense you get that you are watching the real thing is enhanced by the extended interviews with people who actually knew both Reed and Bryant. They all have strong opinions. They are wise. They are insightful. We hear from communists and anti-communists, socialites and politicians, working-class philosophers and credentialed academics. It is a beautiful mix.

From a political perspective, the film offers a devastating turnaround judgment on the results of revolution. Emma Goldman tries to talk some sense into Reed in the years following, and explains that millions have died from starvation, that nothing works right, that the vanguard of the proletariat has become a centralized police state. Reed won't listen. He explains back to her that the socialist revolution requires terror, murder, and firing squads.

Here is the exchange with Maureen Stapleton playing Emma Goldman:

> Goldman: *"Jack, we have to face it. The dream that we had is dying. If Bolshevism means the peasants taking the land, the workers taking the factories, then Russia's one place where there is no Bolshevism."*

> Reed: *"Ya know, I can argue with cops. I can fight with generals. I can't deal with a bureaucrat."*

> Goldman: *"You think Zinoviev is nothing worse than a bureaucrat. The Soviets have no local autonomy. The central state has all the power. All the power is in the hands of a few men and they are destroying the revolution. They are destroying any hope of real communism in Russia. They are putting people like me in jail. My understanding of revolution is not a continual extermination of political dissenters. And I want no part of it. Every single newspaper has been shut down or taken over by the Party. Anyone even vaguely suspected of being a counter-revolutionary can be taken out and shot without a trial. Where does it end? Is any nightmare justifiable in the name of defense against counter-revolution? The dream may be dying in Russia, but I'm not. It may take some time, but I'm getting out."*

> Reed: *"You sound like you are a little confused about the revolution in action, EG. Up 'till now you've only dealt with it in theory. What did you think this thing was going to be? A revolution by consensus where we all sat down and agreed over a cup of coffee?"*

> Goldman: *"Nothing works! Four million people died last year. Not from fighting war, they died from starvation and typhus in a*

*militaristic police state that suppresses freedom and human rights —
where nothing works!"*

Reed: "They died because of the French, British and American blockade that cut off all food and medical supplies. And, counter-revolutionaries have sabotaged the factories and the railroads and telephones. And the people, the poor, ignorant, superstitious, illiterate people are trying to run things themselves just like you always said they should, but they don't know how to run them yet. Did you honestly think things were going to work right away? Did you honestly expect social transformation was going to be anything other than a murderous process? It's a war EG, and we got to fight it like we fight a war: with discipline, with terror, with firing squads. Or we just give it up."

Goldman: "Those four million didn't die fighting a war. They died from a system that cannot work."

Reed: "It's just the beginning EG. It's not happening like we thought it would. It's not happening the way we wanted it to, but it is happening. If you walk out on it now, what does your whole life mean?"

And here we come to understand something of the strange mind of the dedicated communist ideologue, so dogmatic in his adherence to a creed that nothing can shake the faith, not even the deaths of millions and millions of people. His doubts about the revolution and the Communist Party crystallize only when one of his speeches is edited. So, he can turn a blind eye to holocaust, but a violation of his freedom to speak becomes an intolerable act. Some moral compass!

At the same time, we are given a more complicated picture at the ground level of what drove the actual events of the Bolshevik revolution. The film narrative focuses heavily on the Russian war on Germany and what the draft and massive death meant for the Russian people. It prepared them to embrace radical solutions. Lenin, in particular, was more hardcore than anyone else on the need to end the war. In real life, there was another complicating factor here: hyperinflation had also wrecked the economy. Hopelessness is what drove the Russians into the hands of the communists.

Stateside, we discover that World War I, the gigantic military machine erected in the United States to fight it, the betrayal of the antiwar cause by Woodrow Wilson, and the emergence of a capitalist class working together with the state machinery were the issues that emboldened the socialist movement in the United States.

Notice the ease with which the Reds become the Browns. Let's consider militarism, the draft, and the government-business partnership of war to be pieces of what we can call right-wing government. The film brilliantly portrays how the Right prepares the way for the Left (and vice versa)— in both the United States and Russia. The Right gives the motivation and creates the sense of desperation and moral outrage that leads people to embrace utterly implausible solutions like socialism and communism.

And today? After the Soviet Union fell apart, and the system reformed, the regime has backlashed in a different way, still relying on a centralized and despotic state but imposing authoritarian rules on society in the name a reasserted nationalism. We might call the regime what it is: fascist. Notice the ease with which the

Reds become the Browns.

Had there been no war and inflation in Russia, there would have been no revolution, and we would have been spared 80 years of communism. In the United States, the communists and socialists would have remained a small group of activists with no rallying cry, no victim story, no tale of capitalist evil to tell to the public and the workers.

Then and Now

The entire story makes an interesting parallel with our own times. Five years ago, if you had shown me an Obama fanatic, someone for whom this man could do no wrong, no matter how brainless his economic policies or how violent his foreign policies, and I'll show you a person who today hates the guts of Donald Trump–and mostly for the right reasons–but longs for a different form of top-down rule.

The extremists on the right increasing talk just like Jack Reed in the film, longing for "discipline, with terror, with firing squads." We all saw this coming for the last eight years. Obama ruled with an eye to class warfare, breaking functioning markets, harassing business, and alienating the middle class. It was a mix of policies that seemed to be designed to embolden the Left. Then the blowback came with the election of Trump, designed to reverse the flow in favour of a different kind of warfare: the outgroup became the ingroup. And the extremists on the right increasing talk just like Jack Reed in the film, longing for "discipline, with terror, with firing squads."

This process of left-wing statism giving way to right-wing

statism, and back again, provides a summary narrative of the last 100 years of political history. It is a particularly maddening one for old-style liberals and libertarians, since we see how the two work together, often unbeknownst to the partisans, to build the leviathan state step by step.

It is surely not a far-flung hope that someday societies will learn to reject the militarism and regimentation of the Right without embracing the collectivism and violence against property offered by the Left. And someday perhaps there will come a time when the tide of history will turn back the advances of the Left without emboldening the violence of the Right.

In other words, the goal isn't reaction but progress through liberty.

For a century, we've been getting it wrong, and the loss has been missed prosperity and peace. It's time to try a new way.

10

How Much Homogeneity Does Society Need?

It feels strange writing about this topic, some 25 years after I had it completely settled in my mind. But nothing is ever really settled, I suppose. The claim that I had long ago concluded was a basic historical and economic fallacy is back in a big way. The claim is that society needs homogeneity to be orderly and free. It is a core claim of the alt-right and its sympathizers (and, in a different way, of the alt-left). It is what leads them to reject freedom as a path forward and embrace state control of demographics.

It's completely wrong. If you have ever been confronted with this claim, I'm writing this article for you.

Here's the anecdote from my past. Before his death, the now-famous "social nationalist" writer and theorist, and self-proclaimed fascist, Samuel Francis and I were talking at some luncheon. I was prattling on about liberty as usual. And he interrupted me and said, paraphrasing: "Human rights and liberty are slogans we use. Much more fundamental is demographics. You have to have homogeneity for society to be orderly and operate properly. Without that, you can forget about rights and liberties."

Was Francis Right?

Liberty is not the outgrowth of homogeneity. It is the solution to a seeming problem of heterogeneity. I said nothing because I hadn't really thought much about that. Was this right? You don't hear such claims in college. People who talk like this are politically incorrect, and don't say such things in polite company. This thinking leads to forbidden thoughts, and trends toward the celebration of civic sins like racism, sexism, and xenophobia. So I had never really come to terms with it. I didn't have to. But that also meant that I was caught off guard. I sat there a bit confused.

It took a few days but I happened upon a realization. Liberty is not the outgrowth of homogeneity. It is the solution to the seeming problem of heterogeneity. Liberty creates institutions like commercial settings, opportunities for trade and exchange, settings for mutually beneficial trade and learning. It is precisely how liberty reconciles differences among people–and creates wealth out of disagreement–that is the very source of its great magic.

Why is there not chaos? Why is there coexistence? Think back to the end of the religious wars. Enlightenment thinkers proposed that the solution to religious difference is not the burning of heretics and the imposition of an official creed. It was to allow people to believe whatever they wanted so long as they didn't hurt others. And the system worked. How many other ways would this idea of freedom work? Gradually, it came to be rolled out to affect speech, the press, and trade. Eventually it led to broad emancipation of slaves and women. It created a new world, in which the power of the state was restrained and contained and dismantled the old world of imposed hierarchy.

You don't have to know history. Visit the bustling commercial district of any major American city and observe the crazy quilt of ethnicity, language, religion, race, and culture, where people are around buying, selling, and associating according to their own lights. Why is there not chaos? Why is there coexistence? Because the presence of commercial freedom allows everyone to pursue his or her own self-interest in a way that also benefits others. Here is the beauty of the invisible hand at work.

The claim that liberty is preconditioned on the sameness of the population is to wish away the very problem that liberty is much adept at solving. After all, what is the problem that social order is trying to solve? It seeks to provide a setting in which people thrive as individuals even as the entire group is granted an opportunity for a better life. Differences between people are solved by freedom. This was an insight that changed the world for the better.

The trouble is that a homogeneous and isolated tribal unit managed from the top will always be poor. In fact, I realized, if you have a small tribe of that same race, language, religion, and cultural norms, the question of liberty does not have to be raised at all. Group coordination happens due to personal knowledge, verbal communication, and shared expectations of other's similar needs, and it usually features a single leader.

The trouble is that a homogeneous and isolated tribal unit managed from the top will always be poor–mostly living hand to mouth, as small tribes in the Amazon do today–because the model doesn't permit the expansion of the division of labour. It can work under some rarefied conditions. But for the most part, life under imposed homogeneity eventually defaults to what Thomas Hobbes said of the state of nature: nasty, brutish, and short.

The Drive to Integrate

Liberty, on the other hand, rewards ever more integration of people of all kinds. It becomes profitable for everyone to do so. You are free to feel bigotry, racism, loathing of all other religious views, of different lifestyles and so. But when it comes to improving your life, you prefer dealing with the Jewish doctor than having a heart attack, grabbing lunch at the Moroccan restaurant, hiring the Mexican immigrant to tile your bathroom, listening to your favourite African-American pop band, and so on. And guess what? Gradually under these conditions, the primitive and tribalist ethos begins to subside.

This is precisely why any regime that seeks to enforce homogeneity must necessarily turn against the market and toward force. Recall that the Nazi Party had at first only encouraged peaceful boycotts of Jewish businesses, protest signs in front of stores, and so on, and laid out explicit instructions that no one be hurt. That didn't work.

The Nuremberg Laws were a desperate measure to address the "problem" that the market wouldn't work to exclude people.

Or think of the American experience. There was widespread panic about immigration in the late 19th century, not that they couldn't find work but rather than the presence of Jews, Italians, Slavs, and Irish would water down the American race. Wacky theories and policies were unleashed and led to totalitarian measures like forced eugenics, marriage licenses, exterminationist plots against blacks, and so, all justified in the name of realizing homogeneity. The longing for race and cultural purity is frustrated by the existence of freedom and so the next step follows: mass violence.

There is another insight that makes the whole claim about homogeneity a bit silly. As it turns out, no one is the same. And you know this. Think of a friend who shares the same religion, race, language, and sex, and think about your different values. There is always the possibility for conflict because no two people are alike. Your friendships survive despite this because you value your friendship more than being enemies. Expand that model to the whole of the social order and you begin to understand how and why differences lead not to conflict, disorder, and acrimony but rather to friendship, prosperity, and enlightenment.

All this talk of doing away with diversity is a shibboleth. There is no pure race, no truly orthodox religion, no one language without variation, no final unity between any two people in thought, word, or deed. No one acts or thinks as a group or collective. The social world will be, always and forever, a constellation of difference. We need the best possible social system for dealing with and making something beautiful come of it.

The New Realization

I was so pleased to work through the problem in my own mind. As with most intellectual conflict, you end up better off as a result. I came away with a greater appreciation and understanding of what liberty means for the world. Further studies reinforced my conviction that the whole purpose of liberty is to make radical heterogeneity work for everyone.

This is why I became so enraptured by the Convivencia, the 700 period before the High Middle Ages when Islam, Judaism, and Christianity coexisted to their mutual betterment (that all groups benefited from the association is not in dispute, despite the ongoing debate about just how much tolerance for difference there really was).

To understand the awesome power of heterogeneity is to adopt a different outlook on society itself. It is to embrace the core liberal claim: society doesn't need top-down management because it contains within itself the capacity for its own management. You come to be enraptured by Frederic Bastiat's emphasis on harmony as the means by which we live better lives.

The opponents of liberty have been barking up this tree for some 200 years. In contrast, the mental posture that homogeneity is a necessary condition leads to a series of strange obsessions over unending conflicts in society. You begin to exaggerate them in your mind. It seems like you are surrounded by a plethora of intractable wars. There is a war between blacks and whites, men and women, gays and straights, Christianity and Islam, the abled and disabled, our nation and their nation, and so on. This is the very mindset that the left and right have in common.

And guess what? If you build a large state, these conflicts do indeed appear to be more real than they are, simply because the state pits people against each other. You begin to hate that group because its members didn't vote for your candidate, it gets more of the tax loot, it favours various forms of imposition on your liberty. Thanks to this interventionist state, you feel as if you are surrounded by enemies and lose track of the possibility for human understanding.

Freedom and Difference

Let's return to the original claim by Mr. Francis, now widely shared and promoted by the alt-right and its sympathizers. It turns out that this is nothing new. The opponents of liberty have been barking up this tree for some 200 years, as I explain in my new book (*Right-wing collectivism: the other threat to liberty*).

"You have to have homogeneity for society to be orderly and operate properly," Francis says. This claim amounts to a rejection of liberalism itself. So let's correct this. You have to have liberty to deal with the inescapable reality of heterogeneity. It's the longing for sameness that leads to conflict, despotism, and impoverished human lives.

Postscript: for readers interested in the liberal theory of society, its origin and development, I highly recommend the first third of Mises's *Socialism*. Here he formulates a theory of cooperation and what he called the law of association, which are powerful elaborations on the theory of the division of labour. The result is a robust and serious social theory—one that Mises himself never again explained in this degree of depth in any of his works. I personally find it the best explanation of society and property and progress I've read.

11

The Welfare State Should Be Abolished

I was honoured to be the guest speaker of the Yale University Political Union last week, addressing the need to abolish the welfare state. The structure of the union breaks down students into "parties" based on political ideology. The guest speaks and then the students challenge. This is followed by minor speeches and challenges from students. The entire event lasts two hours, and the guest gets the final word.

A word on the students themselves: I was amazed at the erudition, decorum, and adult-like collegiality among them. It seems almost out of some movie I've seen, something set in the 1920s. I'm not entirely sure the students fully realize just how special they are. With a student body like this, I suspected that they learn more from engagement with each other than from their classes. Several students confirmed this. And, to be clear, this was true regardless of political outlook.

I, of course, was speaking on behalf of the pure free-market position on the welfare state, going further even than F.A. Hayek to say that the whole thing ought to be scrapped. There is nothing that the welfare state contributes to our lives that couldn't be replaced by the normal operations of the market and civil society. In the end, I lost the debate, two to one, which is not a surprise, but I hope I planted plenty of seeds of doubt about the merit of the welfare state.

Command and Control

This whole topic is widely misunderstood. People think of the welfare state as a system of redistribution to help the poor improve their lot in life. Those who oppose it, we are told, are greedy advocates for the interests of the rich.

My contention is that this is just a story we tell ourselves that has nothing to do with the history and current reality of the welfare state. The welfare state is a system of command and control, imposed by the political elites, that targets politically marginalized groups in a way that, through both bad and good intentions, excludes them from participation in mainstream society.

The grim history is undeniable. Going back 100 years, controls on wages, working hours, marriage, migration, and professions were heavily influenced by eugenic and white supremacist ideology and pushed forward with the intention to mould population demographics in a way approved by political elites.

Where do we get this idea that the welfare state is designed to help people live a better life? This is not the story anyone is taught in class. Mostly this history is suppressed, especially by champions of the welfare state. We are supposed to believe that the purpose of the welfare state was to help people. But I explained that the US already had a huge and growing structure of private welfare in place, particularly as provided by religious institutions dedicated to helping widows, orphans, and new immigrants.

A great example is Mother Cabrini of the Missionary Sisters of the Sacred Heart of Jesus. They opened orphanages all over the East and West Coasts, managing hundreds of properties including hospitals and schools. But for the "Progressive" intellectuals of the period, these institutions were considered unprofessional and entirely too undisciplined, and they sought to displace these institutions with secular and publicly funded services. They succeeded.

Between 1905 and the mid-1930s, the welfare state was built and came to replace private provision. Funding sources dried up following the double blow of the income tax and estate tax, together gutting the fortunes that had been so generous to charitable institutions. Public provision did not make up the difference. But the big change was regulatory. A great example of early efforts is the minimum wage. When it was first presented, it was designed not to raise the wages of the poor but to raise the bar of entry into the workforce as high as possible so as to exclude "unfit" portions of the population.

The same story can be told about maximum hours legislation, immigration restriction, marriage licenses, public schools, business regulation, and so much more. The rationale was slightly different in each case but the main goal was the same: to control and manage the population through coercion.

Where do we get this idea that the welfare state is designed to help people live a better life? It began to emerge during the New Deal, but that was just a cover. The New Deal was really about creating large-scale business cartels. The story repeats itself: the people who construct and manage the institutions of the welfare state are not the poor; they are privileged intellectuals working with power elites in industry and government. It has always been so.

Not What We Think

Consider food stamps. These aren't for the poor. But let's look today at the workings of the modern welfare state. The idea that it actually helps the poor is unsupportable. It is funded by vast payroll and excise taxes that harm the poor and middle class disproportionately (the rich pay most of the income taxes). Of the more than $1 trillion of spending that today constitutes what people call the welfare state, most of the dollars end up in the hands of the cartelized medical industry, which results in higher prices, less competition, and lower quality service.

There is a reason why obtaining medical insurance and service is so difficult as compared with buying groceries or software. It is precisely because of so much state involvement. It has ended up restricting, not expanding, access.

Or consider food stamps. These aren't for the poor. The program is administered by the Department of Agriculture to create a guaranteed market for big agriculture. Imagine if the big three automakers could back "car stamps" so that taxpayers were forced to pay for cars for people in a certain demographic. It's nice work if you can get it.

I concluded my speech by calling for a complete end to the welfare state as a necessary part of ending the hegemonic control by the ruling class. If you want to see what the state really does to the poor, visit the traffic court, the jails, the prisons, or see how policing works in poor communities. The state is not the friend of the poor.

The Responses

As you can imagine, my presentation confounded many of the people on the left–which probably constituted fully two-thirds of the people present. Following my speech, speaker after speaker pleaded for the need for the state to take from the rich and give to the poor as if this had never been tried. It's like a narrative that some minds just cannot shake, despite all the evidence.

Still, I found their speeches fascinating because of the pervasive mistakes in their thinking.

Not one speaker on the left seemed particularly interested in the real history and experience of the welfare state as it has been practiced. First, not one speaker on the left seemed to connect the issue of poverty alleviation with the solution of wealth creation. Failing to address the issue of where wealth comes from–the zero-sum mindset here is pervasive–they have yet to learn the basic lesson that Adam Smith tried to explain two and a half centuries ago. He explained that wealth comes from the expansion of the division of labour, trade, innovation, and a flourishing commercial society. The dramatic decline in poverty around the world over the last 20 years comes not from more welfare but from expanding markets.

Second, not one speaker on the left seemed interested in the problem of granting the state power over people's lives, which is very strange. An underlying assumption of their comments was that the state is a benevolent institution that is wise enough to pass and implement legislation that promotes social justice. It seems to be completely lost on these people that political establishments operate according to self-interest and end up advancing themselves most of all. Certainly, no state is interested in the precise political vision of Yale students.

Third, not one speaker on the left seemed particularly interested in the real history and experience of the welfare state as it has been practiced. Indeed, they seemed unwilling to defend any aspects of the status quo, even though policy has been striving for 100 years to implement precisely what they claim to favour. Why the lack of interest in the failures of the past? I suppose it is somewhat analogous to how today's socialists are uninterested in the history of the Soviet Union or Mao's China.

Welfare, Diversity, and Fascism

In my concluding remarks, I drew attention to the complex political dynamics between welfare and diverse population groups living under the same regime. People genuinely resent having their money taken and transferred to groups with which they feel no integral relationship. The welfare state, then, ends up exacerbating religious, racial, gender, and language conflicts, giving rise to populist movements that trend fascist. The advocates of the welfare state bear some responsibility for the rise of authoritarianism around the world.

These remarks were obviously unwelcome by the "social justice" crowd in attendance. Though I faced a lot of opposition, I do have to credit the students for not shutting me down and instead keeping the debate civil. As I mentioned, I was voted down by a margin of 2 to 1, but my hosts were thrilled with this result.

> Your speaking appearance yesterday evening at Yale was memorably phenomenal! I was so very grateful for all of the substantive content and energetic explanations which you provided to our Yale Political Union assembly! Having brought in [other speakers], I can say proudly that in terms of intensive argumentation you topped the list!
>
> In my perspective your arguments at yesterday evening's debate were unrivalled; none of the opponents of your views who spoke during the debate actually provided convincing ideas and arguments that could match your own....This afternoon you were the subject of many campus conversations.

This is what it is all about: advancing good ideas, furthering the conversation, promoting engagement, and encouraging people to rethink the ideologies of top-down social management.

I had a wonderful experience. In some way, I lived my dream: to advocate the abolition of the welfare state at one of the places where the ideology of welfarism was born.

About the Author

Jeffrey Tucker
Editorial Director
American Institute for Economic Research
https://www.aier.org/staff/jeffrey-tucker

Jeffrey Tucker is a former Director of Content for the Foundation for Economic Education. He is the Editorial Director at the American Institute for Economic Research, a managing partner of Vellum Capital, the founder of Liberty.me, Distinguished Honorary Member of Mises Brazil, economics adviser to FreeSociety.com, research fellow at the Acton Institute, policy adviser of the Heartland Institute, founder of the CryptoCurrency Conference, member of the editorial board of the Molinari Review, an advisor to the blockchain application builder Factom, and author of five books, most recently *Right-Wing Collectivism: The Other Threat to Liberty, with a preface by Deirdre McCloskey* (FEE 2017). He has written 150 introductions to books and more than ten thousand articles appearing in the scholarly and popular press. He is available for press interviews via his email.

www.ingramcontent.com/pod-product-compliance
Lightning Source LLC
Chambersburg PA
CBHW031523270326
41930CB00006B/503